an essential guide to
SINGLISH

Illustrations by Miel

ISBN 981-04-6708-7

an essential guide to
SINGLISH

Illustrations by Miel

Gartbooks

First published in Singapore 2003 by Gartbooks,
43-D Beach Road, Singapore, 189681

PUBLISHER   William J Gartshore
PROJECT EDITOR   Samantha Hanna
ILLUSTRATOR   Miel Prudencio Ma
DESIGNER   Randy Lee

Distributed in Singapore by
Gartshore & Associates Advertising Pte Ltd,
43-D Beach Road, Singapore, 189681

ISBN 981-04-6708-7

Typeset in 10pt Futura Book
and printed in Singapore by National Photo Engravers

CONTENTS

FOREWORD

Okay lah…

This book offers words and phrases to non-Singlish speakers who want to spice up their conversations with locals. It is also for all Singaporeans who want to have a laugh at the everyday comedy and wordplay they have created in Singlish. Their language has inspired hilarious cartoon illustrations by Miel, one of Singapore's best-loved and award-winning artists. To appreciate the unique linguistic characteristics of Singapore one really ought to try speaking Singlish. It's easy to learn, but more importantly it's an awful lot of fun! Speaking Singlish will enhance visitors' experiences of dining out, shopping, and getting about town. On a more profound level, understanding Singlish parts a cultural curtain that sheds light on the intellection of Singaporeans. Additional chapters offer tips for bargaining and buying, and information at-a-glance about food, festivals, customs, and things to do.

So make the most lah!

William J Gartshore
Publisher

INTRODUCTION

Singlish is the informal, spoken Asian English indigenous to Singapore—a language academics call 'Singapore Colloquial English'. Most Singaporeans are multi-lingual and speak Singlish as a second language to Chinese and Malay dialects, Tamil, or Standard English. Standard English grammar rarely applies to Singlish. Grammatical endings, tenses, plurals, and the definite article are ignored for the most part, allowing for a more direct rhythmic discourse. Particles and sentence endings feature in Singlish and can be heard in most conversations. "Okay lah" is one example in which 'lah' lends emphasis and conveys a sense of agreement. Economy is the order of the language, with sentences pared to cardinal simplicity. The diction is somewhat chopped, and the intonation has a sing-song quality to it drawn from indigenous Chinese and Malay cultural influences. Singlish is a form of national heritage and a linguistic treasure in its own right. With just a few words it can be spoken in no time!

* Some words marked by an asterisk may be considered coarse and in some cases offensive. These are not recommended for use by non-native Singlish speakers even though some Singaporeans spice their conversations with them.

SINGLISH to ENGLISH
A - Z

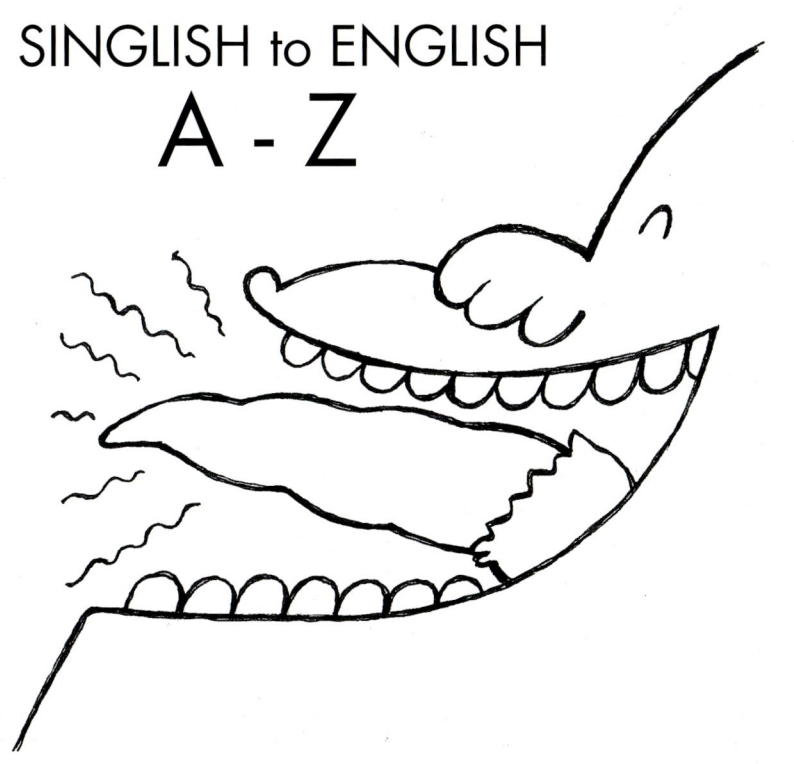

A

Action

To show off.
Example: "See that girl always like to *action*. Always dancing on top of the bar at Carnegie's bar so everyone looking."

Ah beng

A name given to Hokkien-speaking males who have poor fashion sense and behaviour.
Example: "Wah liao, that man so *ah beng*! Somebody should tell him take off that ugly shirt he wears lai dat."

Ah lian

A name given to Hokkien-speaking females with equally poor fashion sense.
Example: "Check out her five-inch platform shoes! So *ah lian* lai dat."

Ah (ber) then?

A rhetorical question that implies one is an idiot for not seeing the obvious.
Example:
Ah beng: "You need to finish project today but got no computer to work on?"
Ah lian: "*Ah (ber) then*?"

Ang moh: Caucasian

Accuse me

Excuse me.
Example: *"Accuse me*, you have time?
Two o'clock is it?"

*Ah pui

A name given to someone who is very overweight.
Example: "My car too small to take so many people home, especially *ah pui* cannot."

Aiyah

Used to express frustration and general fatigue or impatience.
Example: *"Aiyah*! This restaurant too busy to wait all day for makan."

Alamak!

Exclamation of disbelief.
Example: *"Alamak*! Just start new job, orready got retrenchment."

Arrow: pinpoint

Ang moh

Caucasian. In Hokkien, the literal translation for 'ang moh' is 'red hair'.
Example: "Very hot weather *ang moh* cannot tahan. Look his shirt soaking wet."

Arrow

To be charged with an unwanted task.
Example: "Today I leave work early, otherwise I get *arrowed* to write statistics report for my boss."

Ayam

A Malay word that means chicken and is often used in conversation to imply weakness or fear. It is also used when describing someone or something as useless.
Example: "So big 4WD and still driving like *ayam*."
Example: "Why you so *ayam* brand, always fall sick so easily."

B

*Bak chew tah stamp

The literal translation is "eye stuck with stamp/smeared with s**t" and connotes that one is blind.
Example: "You dance with her all night and still cannot see she got hots for you... eh you *bak chew tah stamp*, is it?"

*Balls drop

To feel alarmed or frightened.
Example: "First time I take cable car to Sentosa, so high make my *balls drop*!"

*Bang balls

To feel frustrated or impatient.
Example: "All day try to reason with my client, still not happy with proposal. *Bang balls*, man."

Blur

To describe one who is confused.
Example: "Five times I show you the way to my house and still you cannot find it. Why so *blur*?"
Example: "He so *blur* like sotong. Cannot understand the question, cannot give the answer."

Bo cheng hu

A Hokkien term that means 'without government'. It is used to describe a state of anarchy.
Example: "Teacher not here to supervise class. Today *bo cheng hu* can play games only."

Bo chap

Don't give a damn.
Example: "Boss go on holiday for long weekend. *Bo chap* man, don't bother go to work on time!"

Balls drop: scared

Bo eng lah!

Not available or unable to commit.
Example: "Must study for exams on Friday.
Want to go out but cannot...*boh eng lah*!"

Bo hew

Often used for emphasis. Really don't give
a damn. Couldn't care less.
Example: "Public holiday tomorrow, no need
finish work. Even boss also *bo hew*!"

*Bo ji

Cowardly.
Example: "Work so long hours what?
Ask boss for raise. *Bo ji* or what?"

Bo pian

A Catch-22 or no-win situation.
Example: "My wife and mother arguing
again, must keep quiet. *Bo pian*, always."

ELVIS of KATONG

Botak: bald

Buaya: womanizer

Borrow me

Lend me.
Example: "Left my wallet at home man, *borrow me* ten dollars can?"

Botak

Bald or shaven.
Example: "New haircut? *Botak* now, want to look younger is it?"

Buay song

Unhappy.
Example: "You *buay song* ah? She got new boyfriend?"

Buay tahan

Intolerance or impatience. A Hokkien word that implies one can't deal with a problem.
Example: "That guy every time *buay tahan*. Cannot wait his turn for parking space."
Example: "Alamak! New accounting software got so many things to learn and read thick manual, *buay tahan* ah!"

Buaya

Literal translation is crocodile. It is used in fun to imply that someone is a predator. The word 'buaya' refers to men chasing women, and can simply mean 'womanizer'. Example: " He's such a *buaya*, always flirting outrageously. Not safe to talk to him! So *buaya*!"

Sometimes the word is used as a verb, as in *buayaing*, which means to act flirtatiously. Example: "That *buaya* always at this bar on Ladies Night so he can meet new girls, but orready got so many girlfriends, what. Last week I saw him buayaing at Zouk, this week *buayaing* at Bar None."

C

Can

Yes.
Example: "My son asked me if I take him to Sentosa. I said if you finish your homework, can. He asked if I would take him to movies, I said if he cleans his room then also *can*."

Can

A compliment and term used to praise a person.
Example: "You play golf like professional, man. Like Tiger Woods, you very *can*!"

Can I hepch you?

Can I help you? Often used in sales environments.
Example: "*Can I hepch you*? This one have ten per cent discount, also have many colour."

Cao keng

To evade responsibility.
Example: "Mai *cao keng*, you not ill at all!
Go and take the medical test and finish your work first."

Catch no ball

No idea. To misunderstand.
Example: "Don't talk so much about technology, I *catch no ball*, just give me auto focus camera!."
Example: "Eh how many timea I tell you? He cannot speak Chinese, you talk and talk but he *catch no ball*."

Cham siong

An attempt at compromise or negotiation when in a bind.
Example: "I finish my homework tomorrow teacher. Why got detention? Can *cham siong*, I help to clean classroom."

Char bor

Female.
Example: "That *char bor* very powerful. Got high position in the company."

Cha si lang

Noisy. A term that also means: 'loud enough to wake the dead'.
Example: "That building construction next door *cha si lang*. Too much drilling!"

Cheena

A term used to describe old-fashioned Chinese dress, behaviour or attitude.
Example: "My auntie so *cheena*, always dressed up in gaudy red & yellow!"

Chin chye

To be satisfied with any outcome or to be without preference.
Example: "We take the MRT or we take the bus. Still arrive. *Chin chye*, so how?"

Cha si lang: noisy

Chinese helicopter

To be Chinese-educated. Often used to describe people who do not speak English. Example: "You know he's *Chinese helicopter*, then you ask him question in Mandarin lah! Talking English, what for?"

Chio

Gorgeous. Beautiful. Pretty.
Example: "Your sister very *chio*, I like to meet her next time."

Chio bu

Beautiful girl.
Example: "Wah so *chio bu*! That girl make me dizzy, man!"

Chope

To reserve or hold.
Example: "Today is Saturday. Must *chope* tickets for the new movie or too many people and cannot see."
Example: "Can *chope* one seat for me at your table? I come back after."

Choy

A word used to ward off misfortune.
Example:
Ah Beng:"Still watching TV ah! Tomollow you taking test, sure get geelo one!"
Ah Lian:"*Choy!* Don't curse me O.K."

Chuay si

To flirt with death. It is an expression used as a warning.
Example: "Eh *chuay si*, you know nothing about soccer man, but still want to bet on Liverpool is it?"
"Eh this young punk chuay si want to race motorbike but doesn't know the danger for speeding what."

Colour water

Vain or arrogant.
Example: "You see my brother, always *colour water* wearing leather coat in so hot weather man!"

D

Dao

Vain or arrogant.
Example: "Now he has a promotion, get so *dao*."

Diam

Be quiet.
Example: "Why making so much noise? Can you *diam* or not? I want to watch TV O.K.!

Die die

Absolutely. No matter what happens.
Example: "*Die, die* I also must pay my rent by today"

Doe wan

No thank you. (I don't want it.)
Example: "My boss offer me promotion but too much work. Always work on weekend. Promotion *doe wan*."

Don't play play

Don't fool about. Be serious.
Example: *"Don't play play* ah! You want to borrow can, but this camera very expensive lor! "

Dua

To joke with a person who is gullible.
Example: "You *dua* me! You asked me to back Man U when you know that Arsenal will win!"

Dui

To feel joked with or to feel had.
Example: *"Dui*! I should have listened to that other guy and backed Arsenal!"

E

Early don't say

Why didn't you say something earlier?
Example: "Eh, why *early don't say* you can't come? I cook dinner already ah!"

Eh sai?

It's possible?
Example:
Question: "Need to use your bathroom, *Eh sai* boh?"
Answer: "*Eh sai!*"

Eksi

Arrogant or boastful.
Example: "So now he have a new Mercedes, he get very *eksi.*"

Eng

With time to spare.
Example: "Unemployed? You are very *eng* now, ah!"

F

*Fatty bom bom

A fat-bottomed person.
Example: "Move over *fatty bom bom*, so I also can sit down on this sofa."

Fetch

To drive or give a person a lift.
Example: "Shall I *fetch* you to the airport when you leave for your trip?"
Example: "Eh *fetch* me on Friday to your place! I don't have a car and don't want to take MRT."

Fly areoplane

A term used to describe a disappearing act. Often used when one has been stood up.
Example: "You were supposed to fetch me to the job interview by ten o'clock and where? You *fly aeroplane* and then I miss my appointment!"
Example: "Why you *fly aeroplane* so late, now I cannot chope a lift home."

G

Gao keng

One who pretends.
Example: "Always falling in love. Are you really getting married to this man or you *gao keng* only?"

Ga na

A term used whean one is going to have something happen to them.
Example: "My friend buying always credit card and now *ga na* bankrupt."

Geelo

Zero.
Example: "We play the worst soccer team in league and still get *geelo* goal."

Ger

Girl.
Example: "She good *ger*, always visit her mother and bring pandan cake."

Goondu

Stupid.
Example: "Eh *goondu*, why you cannot decide what to eat when set menu only!"

Go fly kite!

Go fly a kite! (Get lost!)
Example: "You want me to do your job as well as mine? Eh, *go fly kite*!"

Go stun/Gostan

Reverse. Used by drivers.
Example: "How to *go stun*? Behind got car!"

Got licence

To have permission.
Example: "Eh I saw you turn off your computer orready. You *got licence* to leave work early is it?"

H

Hah?

What was that? Used to ask a person to repeat a sentence.
Example:a "*Hah*? Speak slow. Can or not?"

Habis

Finished. Used to describe impending doom.
Example: "Oh she *habis* man! Her husband catch her having affair."

*Half past six

Not quite there. Used to describe incompetence.
Example: "That guy have training but still do things *half past six*!"

Hanna

That's enough. Used when one has run out of patience.
Example: Question: "Eh! I ask you so many times can I borrow your car or not?"
Answer: "*Hanna*, okay lah!"

Hao lian

Extreme vanity or arrogance.
Example: "Wah *hao lian*! That ger cannot stop looking at the mirror!"

Happy like bird

Ecstatic.
Example: "She *happy like bird* now she won first prize."
Example: "Ay Henry *happy like bird* that Man U win. Now he collect all his money."

Havoc

A word used to describe a busy, hyperactive person or environment.
Example: "That woman so *havoc*! So old orreade still wearing mini skirt!"
Example: "Don't go there lah. Friday night that supermarket so *havoc*, have to spend two hours plus in line lah."

Heng

A Hokkien word that means good fortune or to have luck on one's side.
Example: "This week very *heng*; teacher delay our exam to next week."
Example: "So *heng* after play play Singapore Sweep lah. I win one thousand over dollars!"

Hero

Hero. Used to describe an attention-seeker.
Example: "Why you working every weekends when the client orready approve our work. Want to be a *hero* is it?"

Hiao

Vain.
Example: "She comb her hair all day that one, so *hiao*!"
Example: "Eh you so old you still want to *hiao*. What for lah? Got marry orready."

How can?

How is that possible? Used to express disbelief.
Example: "Yesterday got paid and today orready no money left! *How can*?"

Hum pah lang

The whole lot.
Example: "I love Great Singapore Sale. First I buy just a few things, then *hum pah lang* take home."

Humtum

To strike a person using one's hand or an object. To hit at.
Example: "Next time you miss school the teacher tells me then you know. I *humtum* you."

Hup ply

Half price.
Example: "If we go to that bar for Happy Hour can get drinks *hup ply*."

I

Ingrish

English.
Example: "How to speak to him when he doesn't understand *Ingrish*?"
Example: "Go holiday to Hong Kong is it? Neh mind, everything also *Ingrish*."

Is it?

A generic question used in various forms. In most cases it appears at the end of a statement. It can also be used to express skepticism. It often takes the place of 'do you?' or 'have you?' and 'is that so?'
Examples: "Going on a holiday to Europe *is it*?"
"Oh, just recently got married *is it*?"
"Like to eat spicy food *is it*?"
"Trying out for Olympic swimming team *is it*?"
"Lucy *is it*?"

Marcus Wilson Ng

J

Jia chua

A Hokkien word that is used to imply a person is lazy.
Example: "All week play solitaire on your computer, *jia chua* ah! I also want to play solitaire but must finish work lah!"

Jia lat!

A term used to imply that a situation is very serious.
Example: "Sure got big phone bill this month. *Jia lat*, talk all night to my friend overseas but how to pay?"

Ji seow

To bother somebody. To be annoying or to behave in such a way as to provoke a reaction.
Example: "Every five minutes that guy calls me. I try to finish my work and still he *ji seow* me all day."

Jambu

Pretty. In Malay this word also means guava.
Example: "Ah look who got new dress! Eh *jambu*. Going out tonight is it?"

Juang

Whatever. Used as an intensifier and to express a lack of will. It is often used to imply that one doesn't care or that one can't be bothered with details.
Example: "If she is spreading rumours about me in the office, *juang* lah, everybody know already she tok kok all the time."
"You get me something to eat for three dollars *juang* lah, I'm so hungry."

Jude

Pretty or sweet.
Example: "That ger very *jude*. Maybe I ask her phone number and send her SMS."

K

Kai kai

A Hokkien phrase that means 'walk walk' and can be used to simply mean 'go out'. Example: "They went to Orchard Road. *Kai kai* and probably spend too much money."

Kan cheong

To hurry while flustered or uptight. Example: "Why so *kan cheong* when the boss haven't give deadline yet?"

Kang kor

A Hokkien term meaning bothersome or uncomfortable. Example: "I give you one simple job but still *kang kor* and did not finish!"

Kapoh

To steal or to grab. Example: "If I see any leftover food I *kapoh* one bottle for you."

Kaypoh

A nosey person. One who meddles.
Example: "She so *kaypoh* always asking too many personal questions."

Kayu

Stupid.
Example: "Uncle, you so *kayu*. Still gambling but never win, is it?"

Kelong

A name for wooden foundations built into the sea and used for fishing. The term is used to describe some form of sabotage or corruption in the context of a competition. It is often used in reference to sport.
Example: "Wah! Germany 8, Saudi Arabia Geelo, this match sure *kelong* lah!"

Kena

To receive something unpleasant.
Example: "You *kena* big smack if you don't be quiet!"

Kaypoh: nosey

*Kena sai

To be stained by s**t. Used to describe one who is a disgrace.
Example: "That guy! *Kena sai* what, dancing so drunk lai dat..."
Example: "Eh *kena sai* ah! Stop making so much noise O.K. My children sleeping you know!"

Kiam chye

Pickled vegetables. A term used to describe crumpled papers.
Example: "Look at your files so *kiam chye* after you spilled your coffee is it?"

Kiam pah

To be owed a beating. It is used to describe one who is asking for trouble.
Example: "Be careful, *kiam pah* ah!
Can never borrow her car without asking first lah."
Example: "Eh *kiam pah*! You want to have a fight what? My boss find out I give you a key to his office and then you know!"

Kiasu

Kiasu: always wanting the upper hand

Kiasu

BUFFET
ALL YOU
CAN EAT

Kiasu: afraid to lose out to others

*Kiam siap

Miserly or mean. Used to describe one who is uncharitable.
Example: "Don't like that so *kiam siap* and never give your seat to the old woman."

Kiasee

Afraid to die. Used to describe one who always fears the worst.
Example: "You always so *kiasee*. Never can say yes or no, always want to see first lah."
Example: "Eh what for you are too *kiasee* to take cable car? Scared of the sky is it?"

Kia si lang

To be scared to death.
Literal meaning: Giving the dead a fright!
Example: "Next time drive slowly! Auntie so *kia si lang*, nearly got heart attack orreadly."
Example: "Eh you got white face. *Kia si lang*, see your credit card statement is it?"

Kiasee: afraid to die

Kiasu

Afraid to lose out to others. Always wanting the upper hand or something for free. Example: "Look at him so *kiasu* pushing people away to get a seat on the bus first."

Kilat

Smooth or polished. Used to describe anything that is impressive and classy. Example: "That new bar so *kilat* all the celebs going there."

Koon

Sleep.
Example: "Very tired lah. Now must *koon*. Wake me after one hour."

Kopi

Coffee.
Example: "Come let's go buy *kopi* first, then back to work some more."

Kopi tiam

Coffee shop.
Example: "See you for makan at the *kopi tiam* next door."
Example: "Want to come join me and my friend at the *kopi tiam* in Balestier Road? Have kaya toast. It's very delicious."

Koyak

Ruined or broken.
Example: "This DVD player *koyak*. Have to buy new one."
Example: "What for borrow his car when damn *koyak* man?"

Koyok

Doubtful quality. The term is used to describe cheap and nasty products.
Example: "Very cheap washing machine to buy because *koyok* lah."

L

Lah

'*Lah*' is the salt of Singlish dialogue, an indispensable utterance sprinkled with generosity onto the language. At the same time, it is used to pepper all sorts of sentences. More often than not, it is employed at the tail end of a shorter sentence to underline meaning or place emphasis. It is used to convey acceptance, understanding, affection, lightness, jest, and a medley of other positive feelings; it is seldom associated with negative emotions. Sometimes, it is used as a tag word with no particular meaning at all. It is most often heard as "okay lah" and carries a sing-song quality that lifts the phrase.

Examples: "Don't know what to do *lah*!" "Hurry up lah. I want to go home *lah*." "Where we go for makan today *lah*?" "Okay lah, I be more careful *lah*!"

Other popular endings include '*leh*' and '*lor*'.

Leh

'*Leh*' is a suffix used in an enquiring manner. Sometimes it is used to convey a sense of surprise.
Examples: "I never knew he had so much money *leh*. He retired lai dat at 40 years old only!"

Lor

'*Lor*' is another suffix that tags the end of a sentence in much the same way as 'lah'. There are however, shades of variation in the nuances. 'Lor' is not quite as positive as 'lah'; it carries a tinge of cynicism, conveys a mild disappointment or expresses a resigned attitude. Sometimes it is a more lethargic version of 'lah'.
Example: 'So much space he don't use what and don't want to share? Neh mine, he always lai dat *lor*.'

Sentence Endings...

Can ah?   Can you or can't you?

Can lah   Yes.

Can leh   Yes. Of course.

Can lor   Yes. I think so.

Can hah?   Are you sure?

Can hor   You *are* sure then...

Can meh?   Are you certain?

Lai dat

Like that.
Example: "Take that shirt off. Want to look stupid *lai dat*?"
Example: "You *lai dat* anyhow play golf! It got its own rules you know!

Langar

To collide with.
Example: "Eh drive straight, otherwise kena *langar* somebody."

Lau pok

Lousy or no good.
"Don't want to use this old mobile phone, so *lau pok*."

Lau yah pok

Broken or useless. Not worthy.
Example: "This photocopy machine *lau yah pok* already. Company must buy new one."

Longkau chui

Drain water. A term used to describe weak or poor tasting drinks
Example: "Send this back lah! This coffee taste like *longkau chui*, make me want to vomit."

Look see

To take a look. Browse.
Example: "Come let's go *look see* at the new food court. Got many set menus."

Lose face

To lose dignity.
Example: "Don't ask me to explain difficult technology to client. Client knows more technology than me, then I sure *lose face*."

Lost form

To lose one's sense of decorum. Often used when describing an embarrassing situation.
Example: "Eh fall down stairs like that make me so *lost form*. Everybody laughing at me lai dat."

M

Ma fan

To bother or annoy.
Example: "My children like to *ma fan* me when I have work to do!"

Macam

Like. From Malay and used when drawing comparisons.
"Your car *macam* drive like tank man, so slowly what."

Mai

Don't. From Hokkien.
Example: "*Mai*, never mind lah, no need chair, I can stand."

Mai siao siao!

Don't be crazy!
Example: "How to fix electric wires when your not electrician? *Mai siao siao*! Your want to kill yourself is it?!"

Main

Play. From Malay. Used to describe being fooled, cheated, or having been played in some way.
Example: "Don't buy a car from that guy, you kena *main* by him like me what."

Main control

To simultaneously control a number of tasks.
Example: "So many assignments for school, must have *main control* before exams."

Mai tu liao

Don't waste time.
Example: "This shop close in half hour then finish sale orready. *Mai tu liao*! Everything must buy."

Makan

Eat.
Example: "Eh, Newton Circus very good place for *makan*."

Mana eh sai

How can this be? Used to express disbelief.
Example: "Got brand new car, what.
Cannot start engine. *Mana eh sai*?"

Mana oo eng

I don't have time. I'm not free.
Example: "Too much work for makan,
mana oo eng."

Mm sam mm say

Neither here nor there.
Example: "This construction project *mm
sam mm say*. Renovation can, demolish
also can."

Mm chai si

No fear of death. No fear of
consequences.
Example: "Why you talk rudely to the
teacher lai dat, *mm chai si*, is it?"

ma-
ka n

Makan: eat

Shiok: exceptionally good

Newton Circus

Years ago, hawkers cooked their food in the streets using a small permanent cooking station with basic utensils. Some hawkers were mobile vendors. Today, hawkers operate in food centres and still offer the range of cuisines they did in the old days. Newton Circus is arguably Singapore's most famous hawker centre, located in Scotts Road just opposite Newton MRT station. This busy food market is open 24 hours every day, though some stalls don't set up until late afternoon. The best time to visit is in the evenings when hawkers are busy cooking and the atmosphere is buzzing. It can become crowded even after midnight when nightclubbers drop in for a meal. There is a good selection of seafood and local dishes. Prices tend to be higher than other hawker centres but the food is 'shiok', including the barbecued stingray served on a banana leaf.

Eating out 'old Singapore-style' is the real treat when visiting hawker centres. It's a good idea to walk around the entire place first to check out the many stalls that are cooking up a storm. When placing an order, tell the hawker your table number or point in the general direction of where you are sitting. Pay for your food when it arrives.

N

Nah

Here. It is used when passing objects between people.
Example:"Where my pen, ah?"
"*Nah*, take it. I fininsh orready."

Neh mine

Never mind. It doesn't matter.
Example: "Not finish yet? *Neh mind*. Finish tomorrow lah."

Never see before

So what? Have you never seen this before?
Example: "She got belly button pierce. *Never see before* meh?"

No more orready

Run out. To be out of stock.
Example: "Size tree don't have. *No more orready*."

No nid

No need. Not necessary.
Example: "Got passport to Sentosa?"
"Eh *no nid* passport to visit Sentosa."
"Eh Rohani you cold is it? Want to off the aircon?"
"*No nid*, I'm leaving soon."

No stock already

We don't have it in stock.
Example: "Want to buy other colour. Red one have?"
"Red one cannot. *No stock orready*."

Norchet

Not yet.
Example: "Eh finish work or not?"
"No. *Norchet*."
Example: "Your husband back from business trip to Shanghai?"
"Husband *norchet* come back. Maybe tomorrow lah."

Obiang

Ugly or inappropriate. Unattractive.Often used to describe unfashionable dress.
Example: "Uncle please don't wear lai dat, so *obiang*. Come let's go buy new shoe."
Example: "That girl wear too much makeup. Why she want to look so *obiang*?"

Off

Turn off.
Example: "Can *off* the light for me please?" or "Want to go home but must *off* my computer first."

Orready

Already.
Example: "She *orready* finish her exam what. Graduation next lah."

On

Turn on.
Example: "Please *on* the printer." or
"Want to make tea must *on* the jug first."

Orleng joo

Orange juice.
Example: "Don't want lime joo,
want *orleng joo*."

Orso can

Also can – or that is also possible.
No problem.
Example: "This software use for PC,
but Macintosh *orso can*."

Over orready

To run out.
Example: "Nasi lemak no more.
Breakfast only. *Over orready*."

P

*Pai kia

Bad boy. From Hokkien. Used to describe troublemakers.
Example: "He study before but now cannot. All day going with that other one *pai kia*."
Example: "Now he is getting into more trouble with the law, too many problem and cannot go straight because he is always stealing, lai dat so *pai kia*."

Pai seh

Forgive me (apologetic). Also used when feeling embarrassed.
Example: "Every day this week you fetch me to work, *pai seh*. I return a favour to you soon."
Example: "*Pai seh*, I forgot your name. Soorry ah. Can repeat again?"

Pak kiew

To hit the ball. From Hokkien. It is used when referring to sports.
Example: "Want to *pak kiew* next week? Got new golf clubs, must learn to use lah."
Example: "Eh if Man U learn to *pak kiew* properly then maybe I place bet on them lah.
I no stupid, I bet on Arsenal only."

Pang seh

To be stood up.
Example: "Again *pang seh* after I buy tickets to movie. I never ask her to come again."
Example: "Eh I never do lai dat *pang seh* my mother. I take her to church every weeks. Must show some respect lah."

Pecah

Broken. From Malay.
Example: "My car cannot borrow you lah, *pecah* already."
Example: "Wah put so much weight after Chinese New Year. Scared or not you *pecah* this chair?!"

Pergi

To go.
Example: "Eh *pergi* lah. Show starts in fie minute lah."

Punchan

Reprieve. To give someone a second chance or small advantage.
Example: "Okay your work not finish today lah, can *punchan* you. Tomorrow must finish."

Q

'Q'

Queue. Perhaps the only 'Q' word in the Singlish language is the word 'Q'(ueue). An inherently Singaporean trait, queueing illustrates the state of simplistic orderliness that Singaporeans are known to abide by. Some of the most popular 'Qs' to be found in Singapore are at Changi airport, at the Takashimaya taxi-stand, and on Orchard Road at Robinsons.

Example: "Wah liao, 'q' so long, what! Neh mind, catch MRT better."

R

Relak

Relax.
Example: "Henry, you need to *relak* lah. Work so hard for what? You can die like that."

Rojak

Salad. *Rojak* can be a salad of vegetables and fried snacks served with a sweet spicy sauce. The term also refers to something being a mixed of different elements.
Example: "Singapore people so *rojak*. All many different cultures and languages."

S

Sa kah

To flatter someone or win their favour.
Example: "I can tell you want promotion but why *sa kah* so obvious lah!"

Sabo

Sabotage.
Example: "Why you change my work after I leave the office. Trying to *sabo* me or what?"

Sayang

Such a pity! Wasteful.
Example: "*Sayang ah*! I so sure that team would win but I didn't bet on them."
Also means to love. From Malay. It is often used to console children.
Example: "*Sayang* lah, I take care of you."

Salah

Wrong.
Example: "You *salah* about those dates orreadly now. We cannot buy tickets until next week."

Sart

Invincible.
Example: "You pass every test, you very *sart*. How you can study lai dat?"

See gin nah!

Translates as 'die children', from Hokkien. '*See*' means die and '*gin nah*' means children. The term is used when scolding someone.
Example: "*See gin nah*! I give big smack and then you know!"

Seik bai

Failure. Used to describe a failure or a loser.
Example: "He is definitely *seik bai*. Give him map and still cannot find my place."

See beh

Very. Gives emphasis to various Singlish words.
Example: "*See beh* blur! Too many instruction in this manual, how to fix this DVD man..?"

See first

To adopt a wait-and-see approach. The term is used when someone is reluctant to make a commitment.
Example: "Don't buy ticket for tonight. *See first*, lah. Maybe something cheaper also can do."
'*See first*' is considerd a kiasu trait. People who '*see first*' are waiting for some thing better to come up. "*See first* if she invites me go to her party, otherwise I go his party."

See no touch

Look but do not touch. A warning to others not to handle the merchandise.
Example: "Tell your chilchen *see no touch* ah, this things very expensive okay!."

Seow eh

Term of endearment that means 'crazy one'.
Example: "*Seow eh*, still want to go bunjee jumping ah?"

Shack

Tired. Exhausted.
Example: "So damn *shack* man! Worked 80 hours this week and still got study for exams. This work never finish, is it!?"

Shiok

Exceptionally good. Of a very high standard. The term is often used by Singaporeans when discussing food.
Example: "You want to have really *shiok* prawn mee, then go to Newton Circus first." The term also applies to one's state of being or frame of mind.
Example: "Two weeks holiday in Bali make me very *shiok*! All day relak and go surfing. Shiok, man."

Sian

Bored. Very tired, or sleepy.
Example: "Today very *sian*, got no money cannot do anything, just wait for next day to do something lah."

Siao liao

Crazy or insane. To be out of one's mind. Example: "Alamak! You *siao liao* is it? Want to go water ski but don't know how to swim!" The term is sometimes used to describe a crisis or disaster, or an extreme situation. Example: "*Siao liao*, geelo draw and penalty shoot-out! I sure lose all my money now."

Siong

Difficult or tough-going. The term is used to describe a task or situation that is particularly challenging. Example: "*Siong*, my officer put me on guard duty tonight, and then double shift tomorrow to finish all the paperwork. How can? No sleep lah!"

Sirrus

Serious. Example: "You *sirrus* or not? Dun bluff."

Skarly

Suddenly.
Example: "I drive in left lane and *skarly* that bus come into my lane and smash my lights just lai dat!

So bad one

That's not nice of you..! The term is used to let someone know they are out of line.
Example: "You *so bad one*. Want to make me lose face in front of my boss. Don't lai dat next time!."

Solid siah!

Simply great, superb!
Example: "That Bruce Lee *solid siah*! Only want to watch his DVDs lah."

Sotong

Confused. Sotong is the Malay word for an octopus (whose ink is cloudy and blurs the water, making it difficult to see clearly).
Example: "You orready got a map to guide you! Yet you can't find the zoo? Why so blur like *sotong*!"

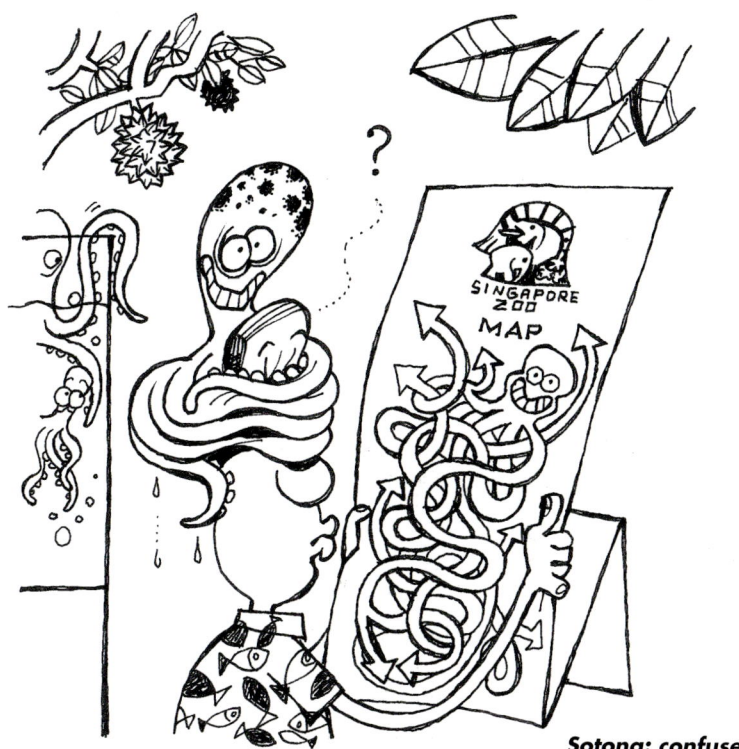

Sotong: confused

Spoil the market

To raise the standard (of something) to an unacceptably high level so that others look bad.
Example: "Now he give free drinks with set menu and *spoil the market*!"

Steady lah!

Good going! Used to compliment someone.
Example: "Eh, *steady lah*, you champion swimmer now what!"

Stylo mylo

Stylish or hip.
Example: "Wah, your new shoe very *stylo mylo*."
The term also describes a cool action or the way something is done.
Example: "You play guitar lai dat so *stylo mylo* man."

Spoil the market: raise standards enough that others look bad

*Suaku

Mountain tortoise. From Hokkien. The term implies one is a simpleton from the country. Example: "Never use internet before? Wah so *suaku*!"

Suan

To insult or mock a person. Example: "Wah! Kena *Suan* man, comparing my dancing with John Trabota!"

Suay

To be down on one's luck. Example: "Ah *suay* leh, four times try out for the soccer team and still cannot play." It can also refer to having a run of bad luck. Example: "She so suay, last week her apartment was robbed and this week she smash her car."

Sup sup sui

It's no big deal. The term is used to describe something as minor and inconsequential. Example: "Two days late *sup sup sui* lah! I can submit my application another time."

Stylo-mylo: hip

T

Tahan

To endure or tolerate.
Example: "I cannot *tahan* the way my supervisor speak to me"

Tan ku

To wait for a long time for something almost too good to be true.
Example: "Eh *tan ku*, you wait long long and then you see Singapore can enter the World Cup!"

Tau tia

Headache. The term is used when referring to an unpleasant or difficult task.
Example: "So urgent! How to meet your deadline? *Tau tia*, everytime you want something last minute."
Example: "Wah so *tau tia*, always changing this one and that one and then the client still did not approve."

Teh tarik   Tea. (Literally means pulled tea.)

Tekan   To be attacked unfairly, picked on or used
                       as a scapegoat.
                       Example: "Cannot go out tonight, got *tekan*
                       by my parents got to stay home and wash
                       my father's car."

Terok   Troublesome.
                       Example: "Try to change my mobile phone
                       number these days very *terok*, man."

Tok kok   To talk rubbish.
                       Example: "You all the time *tok kok* only, say
                       you want to get fit but never go to the gym."

Tok kong   Special or unique. One of the best.
                       Example: "This new digital camera so
                       tok kong."

Tumpang

To ask a favour.
Example: "If you go out then can I *tumpang* some letters to be mailed from post box?"

Tsao

To run. The term is often used in reference to avoiding something.
Example: "Okay guys, already quite late lah so I *tsao* first before MRT close."

Tua kang

To talk big. Boastful. It is used to describe one who exaggerates.
Example: "You talk like thunder but don't see lightning, you so *tua kang*!"

Tum sim

Greedy.
Example: "See that woman so *tum sim*. She can't eat so much but she take a big plate at the buffet no. How many times go back for more dishes when she cannot possibly eat so much!"

Kopi tiam: coffee shop / Teh tarik: tea

Tup pai

Always.
Example: "Henry *tup pai* go to play lottery but never wins ah."

Tzaiy

To be 'in the know' or hip.
Example: "That guy *tzaiy* lah. Always have many contacts in the industry, always know what to do what's going on."

Tzaiy chiu

To have steady hands. The term also refers to being reliable or capable.
Example: If you want digital imaging, must see Derek first he sure *tzaiy chiu*."

Tzaiy si

To know what death is.
Example: "He's camped in the jungle before and got dengue fever. He now *tzaiy si*, he dare not do it again."

U

Ulu

Deserted or empty.
Example: No point to go there after 10 o'clock at night, that bar so *ulu* orready, everybody go home."
The term also means rural and is used in reference to isolated or remote places. Sometimes the term connotes backwardness or a sense of being behind the times.
Example: "Did you eat boneless duck at Buona Vista, you know that place near to Haw Par Villa? You never eat that? Wah you so *ulu*! It's so famous and you never eat that one! How you live in Singapore so long and still so *ulu* you don't know where is Haw Par Villa?" Using the term '*ulu*' can sound derogatory.

V

Very the

Very. It is often used with exaggeration or with sarcasm.
Example: "That girl very the pretty, I like to know her *very the* much but got no chance, so how? Cannot lah."

Very good, very good, who ask you?

Serve youself right. Also used when scolding children, for example..
Example: "All this time you play play and don't listen. I ask you not to climb then you fall down and you hurt yourself, *very good, very good, who ask you*?"
Example: "You ask my advice then you never listen, *very good, very good, who ask you*?"

W

Wah

Wow
Example: "So much money, *wah.*"

Wah liao!

Wow! Exclamation of disbelief. Sometimes used in jest.
Example: "*Wah liao!* So big durian I never saw before."

Wah piang, eh!

What the hell! Often used to express frustration or when scolding a person.
Example: "You want to use my car all the time, *wah piang, eh* take the keys to my house also!"

Wah, so ex one, meh?

My that's very expensive! Or, that's a rip off!
Example: "$50? *Wah, so ex one, meh?*"

Want or not?

Do you want it or not?
Example: "Lime juice. *Want or not*?"

Wenla

When is it? (Unlikely)
Example: "Boss say pay rise soon, but *wenla*."

Wayang

To pretend.
Example: "I know you eat all my durian, don't *wayang* lai dat, ah!"

Whack

To do anything with reckless abandon.
Example: "Cannot anyhow *whack* this assignment, must think first lah."

What talking you?

What are you talking about?
Example: "Free drinks? Eh, *what talking you*?"

Where got?

How can this be? Often used in defence.
Example: "Wear your jewellery? Borrow your clothes? Eh, *where got*?"

Wah liao!: Wow!

Xiam: get out (of here)

X

Xiam

Get out of the way. Leave me alone. It can also mean 'excuse me' in the context that one wants to be avoided (when carrying a bowl of hot soup across a busy restaurant floor, for example.
Example: "*Xiam, xiam*! Hot Water!"
Another meaning for *Xiam* is to take cover (or avoid responsibility).
Example: "Eh, you better *xiam* before boss get back and arrow you to do this monthly report."
Example: "I must *xiam* now otherwise they kick me out, I did not remember the dress code."

Ya ya: show-off

Y

Ya ya

Boastful. Showing off.
Example: "Wah, he so *ya ya* one. He don't know anything and yet he thinks he got good skills to play soccer for Man U!"

Yan dao

Handsome. Nice looking. Dashing.
Example: "My brother so *yan dao*! Got many secret admirers."

Yau gui

Literal: Hungry Ghost. Greedy.
Example: "Wah liao, you so *yau gui* one, everything also must eat."
Example: "My sister so *yau gui*, always snacking and can never fill up."

Z-monster: sleepy

Z

Z-monster

An old army term used to describe being sleepy.
Example:
Sergeant: "Recruit, you must learn to fight the *Z-monster*!"
Recruit: "Sir, yes sir!"
Sergeant: "Even monkeys can fight the *Z-monster*! Where is your weapon?"

Zuo bo

To do nothing. Used in the context of being bored or lazy.
Example: "Today got no money lah, what to do? Just stay home lah, what to do *zuo bo*."

GREETINGS AND CIVILITIES

Hello/Hi.	Eh. Long time no see. Hi.
Good morning.	Hi.
Good afternoon.	Hi.
Goodnight.	Bye.
I'm pleased to meet you.	Nice to meetchu. Hi.
How are you?	So how?
How are things?	Eh how?
I'm well, thank you.	Okay lah.
I'm allright.	Lai dat. So so lah.
I'd like to introduce you to my wife.	This my wife.

What do you do for a living?	What you doing now?
Where are you going?	You go where?
Goodbye.	Bye.
See you later.	Okay lah, ketchup with you.
Have a good trip.	Joy yourself.
Excuse me.	Accuse me.
Please join me.	Come join. Yourn join me?
Let's get going.	Come let's go.
I'm sorry.	Sorry, ah.
I'm very sorry.	Oh don't lai dat, sorry lah.
Forgive me.	Pai seh, pai seh.
Don't worry about it.	Sorright lah, sokay neh mind.
Thank you.	Thank you ah.

You're welcome.	No problem. Sokay.
Is that so? Really?	Oh lai dat ah!?
Give me a moment, please.	You wait for a while ah.
Don't leave just yet.	Don't go back first.

FORMS OF ADDRESS

Uncle	Used to respectfully address a senior man. Often 'uncle' is used to address taxi drivers or foodstall attendants.
Auntie	Used to respectfully address a senior woman.
Yen dao (handsome)	Often used to attract the attention of Chinese Singaporean men. It can also be used in sarcasm.
Lao pun or tao kay (boss)	Used to address men in any retail or service industry when special attention is sought.

Tok kok: talk rubbish

SMALL TALK

MEETING PEOPLE

My name is...	I'm...
What's your name?	Your?
Where are you from?	Where your from? or Your from where?
How long have you been here?	Stay here long time?
Make yourself at home.	Eh, don't shy!
I really like the food in Singapore.	Food in Singapore, damn shiok man!
Shall we meet up tomorrow?	Tomorrow, you what time can?

Do you have a business card?	Got card, or not?
Shall we get a bite to eat?	You join me for makan?
You should meet a friend of mine...	Can introduce you my friend leh...
I don't really understand.	How come lai dat?
How can that be?	What for lai dat?
That's really interesting!	Oh, is it?
Work is fine.	Lai dat lor.
I think you made a mistake.	Neh mind.
Let's have a beer.	Tiger can.

LANGUAGE BARRIERS

I don't speak the language.

Don't know how to speak, what.

I don't understand.

Sorry ah. Can say again?

Can you repeat that please?

Hah?

What is this?

This is what?

Please show me.

Show me how.

How do you say...?

How to say...?

What does it mean?

What you talking?

How does it work?

Eh, how to do?

INTERESTS

I like shopping in Singapore.	Shopping in Singapore very cheap lah.
Do you like music?	You listen to music?
I like karaoke.	I sing karaoke very good.
Do you like films?	You see movie or not?
Do you play sport?	You got play any game?
Do you travel?	You go other place?
Do you like dancing?	You go dancing or not?
Which festival is on at the moment?	Where got festival?

What are you looking at?	See what, see what?
I'm on a budget.	Where got money lah?
I understand.	Oh, lai dat ah!
I can't make it.	Cannoh make-ee.
What are your plans?	So how?
This is very nice!	Eh velly nice one.
Excuse me, where is the washroom please?	Accuse me. Toy-lert?
Diamonds are much cheaper in Singapore.	Singapore laimon cheaper.

I don't mind what we do.	Eh, anything also can.
Is there a problem?	Got problem, ah?
Do you want to get into an argument?	Eh, you want to coral is it?
We can arrange things later.	Confirm later lah.
What are you up to tonight?	Tonight go where?
Do you come here often?	This your hangout?
I really don't know the answer to that?	Got mental block.

Catch no ball: no idea

SHOPPING

Shopping in Singapore is something of a national sport and when it is appropriate to do so bargaining is part of the process. Some of the world's most impressive malls can take a day out of one's itinerary so it's advisable to wear comfortable shoes when on the prowl for a great bargain. Orchard Road is famous for its extraordinary department store Takashimaya, at Ngee Ann City, though there are many other well-known malls along this long shopping strip. Suntec City, Raffles City, and Marina Square have large retail chains as well as boutique stores that carry international brand names.

SHOPPING

Affordable electronics and computer peripherals can be found at Sim Lim Square and Sim Lim Tower. For new releases in computer technology, Funan The IT Mall is worth a visit. Here, one can play with the latest notebooks and gadgets and be sure of an international warranty with purchases. It's important to retain receipts for large purchases. The Goods and Services Tax can often be claimed when leaving Singapore. A great place to bargain for digital cameras and second-hand cameras or photographic equipment is at The Camera Workshop, and some other camera stores around Peninsula Plaza. Be sure to bargain.

SHOPPING

There is great fun to be had browsing the various shop houses in Little India, China Town and along Arab Street. The shops are colourful and packed with fabrics, gold, jade, ornaments and household items. Market stalls set up during important festival times. These are the best places to try authentic local cuisine! For market stalls, Bugis Village sells all kinds of souvenirs as well as clothing and jewellery at very cheap prices. When buying in quantity one can negotiate a further discount. Visit Jim Thompson shops for equisite Thai silk. For made-to-measure suits at a fraction of the price in Europe, most tailors take just a few days to fulfil orders.

SHOPPING

There are so few flea markets in Singapore but those that are worth rummaging through can be found at Clarke Quay each Sunday, and at Tanglin Mall every third Saturday evening of the month. Second-hand clothes, collectibles, memorabilia and handmade items are for sale.

Singapore's biggest sale event of the year happens every June. The Great Singapore Sale is a good time to pick up major discounts on just about anything as most retailers are clearing old stock. This sale lasts at least a month and is heavily advertised. Most of the island's large retailers and shopping malls get involved.

SHOPPING

Most shops in Singapore are open seven days a week until 9pm. Some book shops and CD shops such as Borders, Kinokuniya, Tower Books and Records, and HMV Music stay open later–in some cases even until midnight on weekends. In busier shopping areas money changers are everywhere and it's wise to carry cash for bargaining purposes. Prices are generally fixed in major stores and carry a Goods and Services Tax (+++), but smaller stores are happy to negotiate with genuine customers. For those urgent supplies, most petrol stations are open 24 hours, as are 7-Eleven stores that can be found all over the island on main streets.

HOW TO BARGAIN

Using Singlish when bargaining helps visitors appear less like tourists, making it more likely for them to get a local price! Bargaining is part of the shopping experience, especially when buying electronics or souvenirs. Some locals believe that shopping early in the morning guarantees a great price because it is considered good luck for the retailer to give the first customer of the day a bargain. For the rest of the day, good trade is said to follow. It's poor form to refuse a purchase after negotiating an agreed price and bargaining should always be done in a friendly manner. Sometimes a few jokes and laughter can spice up the fun when bargaining with locals and anyway, it opens up the negotiation process to conversation. It's always worth remembering that humour is a useful bargaining tool. Smile. Carry cash.

How much is this?	This one how much?
That seems rather expensive.	Wah so expensive, ah!
That's more than I wanted to pay.	Cannot afford lah.
The price is just too high.	Wah so ex ah!
I don't have that much money on me.	Money not enough lah!
Can you give me a discount?	How? Got discount or not?
I'll offer you ten dollars.	Ten dollars can?
I don't want to pay more than ten dollars.	Got ten dollars only.
Where was it made?	Made from where?

Would you be prepared to lower the price?	Make lower can consider. Lower some more, maybe can consider.
Can we discuss the price?	Can make cheaper lah?
Can you lower the price?	Cheaper can or not?
If I pay cash can I have a discount?	Pay cash get cheaper lah.
Is this an antique?	Antique is it?
How old it is?	How many years is it?
Is this an authentic one?	Fake one is it?
How can you tell it's real?	Real or not? So, how to see?
I'll go and get more money.	ATM where?

Is there something less expensive?	Got cheaper?
What else do you have for around the same price?	Got other one same price? Neh mind, other one also have?
No thank you, I'm just browsing.	Doe wan lah.
Do you take credit cards?	Visa can?
Yes, I'll take it!	Okay lah! Can.
Thank you.	Xie Xie. Thank you ah.
It's just what I had in mind!	Ah, this one can!
It's perfect. I love it.	Ah can, can! I lurve it.

ORIENTAL GOODS

For antiques and oriental rugs and handicrafts, prices can always be negotiated—even for larger items such as furniture that may require shipping. Dempsey Road is popular for its range of artifacts and furniture from China, Thailand, India, and Iran. Most traders here will happily arrange shipping and packing for buyers from overseas. For an array of traditional medicinal products and an extensive range of ornaments and silk clothing from mainland China, Yue Hwa Chinese Products Store is fascinating to wander around. For visitors arriving in time for Chinese New Year, China Town is a must-see for its huge street markets of food and goods, and for street theatre performances that run until late.

GETTING AROUND

How do I get to Orchard Road?

Orchard? So how?

Can I walk there?

Walking. Can or not?

Can you show me on the map?

Show me.

Is there another way of getting there?

How to go there?

What's the best way to get there?

What fastest way?
What cheapest way?

Where is the bus terminal?

Bus interchen where?

Which way is the train station?

Where MRT?

How often do the trains run?

How often does MRT come?

TAXIS

Where can I get a cab?	Taxi stand where?
Please drive on.	Go straight.
Continue straight along this road.	All the way, go straight.
Please turn left at the next corner.	Uncle, in front turn left.
Please turn right at the next corner.	Uncle, in front turn right.
Go over the traffic lights.	After traffic light.
It's just a few blocks away.	Ah, further up.
I need to go to the airport please.	Changi Airport.

BUS

How far is Orchard Rd? — How long more to Orchard?

Can you tell me when we reach my stop? — You tell me where?

Does this bus go to China Town? — Go China Town or not?

How much is the fare? — China Town how much?

TRAIN

Where is the ticket office? — Where to buy ticket?

What's the best way to buy a ticket? — How to buy ticket?

Is there a day ticket? — Eh, what kind of tickets can I buy?

Is there a weekly ticket? — Eh, what kind of tickets can I buy?

Is there a concession? — Eh, got ticket for tourist?

Boat Quay

EATING OUT

Singapore cuisine is a mix of different cultures and there are various dining experiences to be had–from outdoor food vendors and hawker centres to air-conditioned food courts and fine-dining restaurants. Singapore Chilli Crab is a famous dish and many people visit the East Coast seafood outlets to enjoy this spicy meal. Clarke Quay (next to the river) and Lau Pa Sat (near the CBD) are well-known for satay served with sweet peanut sauce. It is Chinese, Malay, and Indian cuisine that dominates the food scene here. Some of the best vegetarian food can be found in Indian restaurants, and the old colonial high tea is enjoyed in many of the large hotels. Some hotels offer sophisticated champage brunch buffets on the weekends, at very reasonable prices.

CHINESE FOOD

Chinese cuisine includes provincial dishes: Hainanese, Shanghainese, Sichuanese, and Cantonese. Hokkien and Teochew food is popular among the cheaper eateries and hawker places.

Hainanese chicken rice

Steamed or roasted chicken with rice and chilli sauce.

Popiah

Soft flour-wrapped rolls of egg, prawns, bean sprouts, lettuce and radish or turnip.

Carrot cake (Chai tow kueh)

Carrot fried with egg and corn starch in a black bean sauce.

Char kway teow

Flat rice noodles stir-fried with Chinese sausage, egg and clams, in a sweet black sauce.

Black chicken herbal soup

A tonic soup eaten for its nutritious value and to promote one's health.

Chilli crab

Deep fried crab in a spicy thick and sweet gravy.

Kaya toast

Kaya is a sweet coconut spread served with boiled eggs and bread dipped in egg and fried.

Dim sum

Cantonese small dishes of dumplings either fried or steamed, or pastry dishes.

Buddha jumps over the wall

A soup of abalone and sea cucumber.

Ice kachang

Shaved ice dessert sweetened with various toppings including coconut cream, fruit, jelly and corn, or red beans.

Mango pudding

Sweet creamy pudding of mango served cold.

Cheng teng

Barley and bean dessert sweetened with fruit.

MALAY FOOD

Malay dishes are spicy and use various ingredients from the region. In keeping with Islamic standards, the food is *halal* and therefore contains no pork.

Mee siam

Vermicelli hot and sour soup with chilli paste, egg and soya beans.

Nasi lemak

Coconut rice served with fried anchovies, peanuts, egg, cucumber and fried chicken or fish.

Otak-otak

A fish paste wrapped in coconut leaf and cooked.

Mee rebus

Egg noodles with thick spicy gravy, egg and chilli.

Satay

Barbecued kebabs of mutton, chicken or beef served with spicy sweet peanut sauce.

Nasi goreng

Fried rice with prawns and egg and lettuce, seasoned with cumin.

Rendang

Spicy curry of beef, chicken or mutton.

Sambal goreng

Green beans in a curry of coconut, tamarind, beancurd and/or meat.

Kueh

Sweet cakes made from coconut, rice, tapioca and palm sugar.

Bubur hitam

Black rice pudding with coconut cream.

Chendol

Iced drink of coconut milk, jelly, syrup and palm sugar.

INDIAN FOOD

Northern Indian dishes are creamy and rich in flavour and eaten with breads. Southern Indian curries are spicy and served with rice. A classic local dish loved by Singaporeans is fish-head curry which is sweet and spicy hot!

Roti prata

Crispy light fried bread, sometimes cooked with egg, onion and sardines, and served with a curry sauce.

Chapati

Wheat bread roasted and served with dhal.

Naan

A tandoor bread in variations of garlic, butter, mint and plain flavours.

Fish-head curry

Snapper head served in a spicy hot sweet gravy and ladies' fingers.

Biryani

Saffron rice cooked with vegetables and nuts served with meat curry or fish masalas.

Alu gobi   Potato and cauliflower cooked in turmeric.

Keema   Minced beef or mutton gravy eaten with bread.

Murtabak   Prata of meat served with curry.

Vada   Fried lentil doughnuts.

Lassi   Yoghurt drink sometimes flavoured with mango, mint or salt.

Kheer   Rice pudding cooked with milk and sometimes enriched with nuts.

Kulfi   Indian ice cream cooked with pistachio nuts and served with rose syrup.

Gulab jamun   Dessert of cottage cheese dumplings soaked in sweet syrup.

Roti prata: fried Indian bread served with gravy

FRUIT

Tropical fruit in Singapore comes from all over Southeast Asia. Many stalls serve fruits already peeled, and chopped and ready to eat. A selection of fruits can be chosen and served on ice, or skewered on sticks and taken away. Fruits include sweet mango, pineapple, watermelon, papaya, honeydew melon, rock melon, coconut, mangosteen, starfruit, jackfruit, pomelo, rambutan, and banana. Durian is a fruit known for its strong pungent smell that can be off-putting, but it has juicy thick flesh and is used to flavour cakes and ice creams. Blended ice fruit drinks are popular. Along Orchard Road and in most food courts and hawker centres are vendors that sell fresh fruit juices, and some street vendors serve ice cream sandwiches–no, seriously!

CUSTOMS

Many locals eat without cutlery and in some Indian restaurants there may be no cutlery at all. Most places such as these will have a sink nearby for the purpose of handwashing. Only the right hand is used for eating, and fingers don't make contact with the mouth (no licking fingers!). The food is scooped up and into the mouth using one's thumb and fingers and this can be tricky. Not all restaurants will provide serviettes so it is worth carrying a packet of tissues around. When using chopsticks, never point at someone with them nor leave the thin end pointing at a dinner guest after your meal. Never stick chopsticks upright because for Chinese people it signals death, and never try cutting food with them as though they were a knife and fork.

CUSTOMS

Some places will have chopstick rests to the right of the plate, otherwise they can be rested across the edge of the plate. It is customary, when dining in a group, to order dishes to be shared and when doing so there will be serving spoons accompanying each dish so that guests don't use their own.

Hawker centres are lively outdoor eating markets that offer a variety of local dishes at very cheap prices. Stall-holders will often call out or approach a potential customer directly to attract a sale and they are competitive along the East Coast, Clarke Quay, and at Newton Circus. Some will find this method of selling food overwhelming and others will enjoy the excitement. There are no restrictions on where diners sit. Have a good stroll around eyeing the fare before you place an order.

CUSTOMS

It depends on individual stall-holders whether they take orders at tables. In any case, remember that food is most often paid for once it is served. Centres are busy at lunchtimes and tables are often shared.

Visitors will experience the polite Singaporean and the pushy 'kiasu' Singaporean. The latter will often dash for a seat on the train or stand in doorways making it impossible for passengers to alight. Some will knowingly jump a queue and show inconsiderate behaviour such as mobile phone use in the cinema.

Business card etiquette should be observed. People present them in social as well as business circumstances. Offer cards using both hands and have the name facing the recipient. Upon receiving one always accept it with both hands and ponder over it a moment as a sign of respect.

CUSTOMS

It is also polite to ask a couple of questions about the type of work a person does when receiving one. Don't put the card away in front of the person who presented it to you, and always stand when you are given a business card introduction at a dinner table.

When visiting someone's house always remember to take your shoes off before entering. The same applies to entering most places of worship and visitors may enter some religious buildings in Singapore. There will usually be a sign regarding photography and dress code. Never point at Muslims nor expose the soles of your feet to Hindus or Buddhists. Always enter a place of worship with respect. These are not tourist places, though some of them allow guests to wander around inside. Some religious buildings require a form of bathing before entering.

Lose face: to embarrass oneself

CUSTOMS

When entering a Muslim, Hindu, or Buddhist building, shoes must be removed and clothing ought to be conservative. If you are unsure about where you may walk around, ask someone for advice.

Always use the right hand to give items to Indian or Malay people. Keep in mind that among Muslims and Hindus, the left hand is for personal hygiene.

Tipping is not common in Singapore because most hotels, restaurants, taxis, and shops charge a service charge, a government tax and a Goods and Services Tax (GST). (+++ on the bill)

The Chinese concept of face exists in Singapore. To lose face is to disgrace oneself in front of others. Never insult, shame or embarrass another person because they will lose face.

CUSTOMS

Loud or obnoxious behaviour in public is considered rude and those guilty of this type of behaviour also lose face, as do people who express their emotions too easily when losing their patience. Singaporeans are quietly observant. Remain courteous.

As a general rule, avoid touching anyone. A pat on the back may be a friendly gesture in some cultures but in Singapore it may be taken for flirtation and even as aggression. Kissing as a greeting between friends is uncommon.

Pointing with a finger is considered rude so use your entire hand with the palm facing up to draw attention to a person or an object. In business settings, do not sit closer than arm's length from the other person. If you do so Singaporeans may find you intimidating or intrusive.

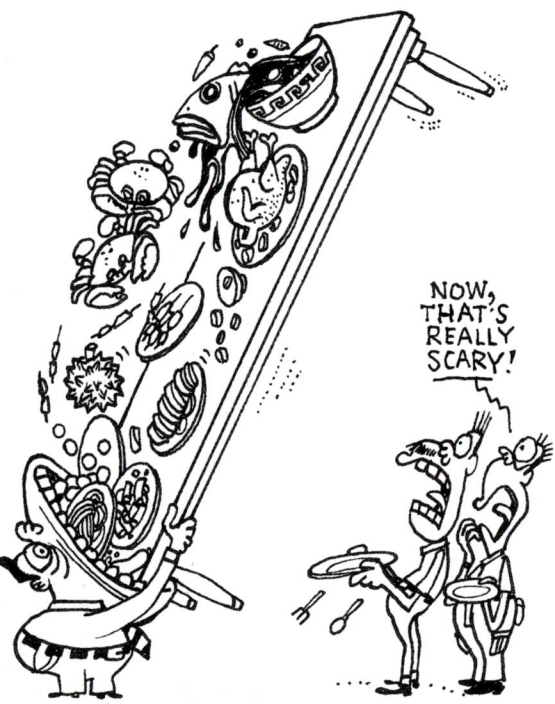

Hungry Ghost Festival: food and prayers are offered to the dead who are believed to return to earth for the seventh lunar month

FESTIVALS

Many of Singapore's festivals are religious and marked by the lunar calendar that changes each year.

Ponggal

Tamil harvest thanksgiving festival is celebrated at Sri Srinivasa Perumal Temple. (Jan/Feb)

Thaipusam

Hindu festival honouring Lord Subramaniam with a procession that includes metal *kadhavis* carried by some worshippers who pierce their bodies with hooks. (Jan/Feb)

Chinese New Year

It is celebrated island-wide, with red (good luck) decorations and lights all over Chinatown. People exchange red packets of money and there are lion dances. Gong Xi Fa Cai! (Wishing you great prosperity!) (Jan/Feb) During this time, the colourful Chingay Parade (mardi gras) takes place in Orchard Road.

Hari Raya Puasa

The Muslim celebration of the end of the holy month of Ramadan. The Sultan Mosque area near Arab Street is filled with food stalls, families dine together and children receive green money packets. (dates vary)

Hari Raya Haji

A Muslim celebration to honour those who have made the pilgrimage to Mecca. A sheep is slaughtered as a sacrifice to Allah.

Vesak Day

A Buddhist celebration in which monks honour the life of Buddha. Temples are filled with prayer and offerings and at night a candlelit procession sets off. (May/Jun)

Singapore Festival of Arts

Drama, dance and music performances island-wide. (Jun)

Dragon Boat Festival and Boat Race

Marina Bay holds the Dragon Boat Race. The festival honours a 4th-century Chinese poet, Qu Yuan, who drowned himself to protest against political corruption.

Hungry Ghost Festival

The Chinese offer food and prayers to dead spirits that return to earth for the seventh lunar month. Incense is burned and Chinese opera and plays take centre stage in the streets. (Aug or Sep)

Mid-Autumn Festival

It is celebrated with mooncakes and lanterns, and honours a 14th-century Chinese patriot who tried to overthrow the Yuan Dynasty. Children carry lanterns to a competition in the Chinese Garden. (Aug or Sep)

Deepavali

The Indian festival of lights is celebrated with spectacular decorations throughout Little India. (Oct or Nov)

Thimithi Festval

Devotees walk barefoot over hot coals and a procession from Sri Srinivasa Perumal Temple to Sri Mariamman Temple takes place. (Oct or Nov)

Nine Emperor Gods Festival

It is celebrated by Taoists who honour the Gods for good luck and for curing illness. A procession takes place and some people make a pilgrimage to Tua Pek Kong Temple at Kusu Island. (Oct or Nov)

Christmas

Orchard Road is decorated with lights and shopping malls erect enormous Christmas trees and fairy tale theme displays. (Dec)

National Day

It is an important public holiday for Singaporeans who celebrate their independence in 1965. The National Stadium hosts parades and cultural performances, and an air show. (9 Aug)

DIRECTORY OF INFORMATION

**Singapore Tourism Board
Tourist Information Centre**
Tourism Court,
1 Orchard Spring Lane,
Singapore
ph: 1800 736 2000

Singapore Visitors Centre
#01-039 Suntec City Mall,
3 Temasek Boulevard, Singapore
ph:1800 332 5066

Police
ph: 999 toll-free
Fire and Ambulance ph: 995 toll-free

Tanglin Police Station
17 Napier Road, Singapore
ph: 6391 0000

Killiney Road Post Office
1 Killiney Road, Singapore
ph: 6734 7899

MAJOR DEPARTMENT STORES AND SHOPPING CENTRES

Isetan
Shaw House,
350 Orchard Road,
Singapore
ph: 6733 1111

Marks & Spencer
Wheelock Place,
501 Orchard Road
ph: 6733 8122

Metro
Paragon,
290 Orchard Road,
Singapore
ph: 6835 3322

Robinsons
Centrepoint,
176 Orchard Road,
Singapore
ph: 6733 0888

Seiyu
Parco Bugis Junction,
230 Victoria Street, Singapore
ph: 6223 2222

Suntec City Mall
3 Temasek Boulevard, Singapore
ph: 6333 6864

Takashimaya
Ngee Ann City, 391 Orchard Road,
Singapore
ph: 6738 1111

Tangs
310-320 Orchard Road, Singapore
ph: 6737 5500

Wisma Atria
435 Orchard Road, Singapore

MARKETS

Bugis Village
Victoria Street, Rochor Road and
Queen Street, Singapore
ph: 6837 0930

Clarke Quay
3E River Valley Road, Singapore
ph: 6337 3292

**Dempsey Road
(Furniture) Market**
Dempsey Road, Singapore
(off Tanglin Road)

Holland Road Shopping Centre
211 Holland Avenue, Singapore
ph: 6468 5334

Tanglin Mall
163 Tanglin Road, Singapore
ph: 6736 4922

ELECTRONICS STORES

Boon Hi-Tech Superstore
#03-29 Raffles City,
252 North Bridge Road,
Singapore
ph: 6339 3421

Lucky Plaza
304 Orchard Road, Singapore
ph: 6235 3294

Mustafa Centre
145 Syed Alwi Road, Singapore
ph: 6298 2967

Sim Lim Square
1 Rochor Canal Road
ph: 6332 5839

The Sony Gallery
#03-30G
Parco Bugis Junction,
200 Victoria Street, Singapore
ph: 6837 0646

COMPUTER STORES

Best Denki
#05-01/05, Ngee Ann City Podium,
391 Orchard Road, Singapore
ph: 6835 2855

Challenger Superstore
#06-00 Funan The IT Mall, Singapore
ph: 6339 9008

Funan The IT Mall
109 North Bridge Road, Singapore
ph: 6337 4235

The Mac Shop
#04-11 Funan The IT Mall, Singapore
ph 6334 1633

Sim Lim Square
1 Rochor Canal Road, Singapore
ph: 6338 3859

Sim Lim Tower
10 Jalan Besar, Singapore
ph: 6295 1176

CAMERA STORES

The Camera Workshop
#01-31 Peninsula Shopping Centre,
3 Coleman Street, Singapore
ph: 6336 1956

Cathay Photo
#01-07/08 Peninsula Plaza,
111 North Bridge Road, Singapore
ph: 6338 0451

John 3:16 Photo Supplies
#03-37 Funan The IT Mall,
109 North Bridge Road, Singapore
ph:6337 1897

Prime Camera Centre
#01-31 Peninsula Shopping Centre,
3 Coleman Street, Singapore
ph: 6336 1956

Ruby Photo
#01-01 Peninsula Shopping Centre,
3 Coleman Street, Singapore
ph: 6338 0236

KARAOKE BARS

BMB Karaoke Box
#03-31 Parco Bugis Junction,
200 Victoria Street, Singapore
ph: 6338 7069

Eddie's Bar
45 Tras Street
ph: 6323 7055

Joy Luck Club
65 Tanjong Pagar Road, Singapore
ph: 6323 7654

Happiness KTV Lounge
155 Joo Chiat Road
ph: 6440 1059

Ming's Café & Pub
195 Upper Thomson Road, Singapore
ph: 6251 3187

My Place Entertainment
4 Lorong Telok, Singapore
ph: 6536 5312

Popular KTV Lounge
750 Upper Serangoon Road
ph:6282 0073

Prince KTV
67 Beach Road, Singapore
ph: 6339 2668

Studio East
8 Grange Road, #09-01 Cineleisure
Orchard, Singapore
ph: 6836 2100

Violet Karaoke
4 Maju Avenue, Singapore
ph: 6283 8422

ISLAND HIGHLIGHTS

Sentosa

An adventure theme park and beach attraction, it has hotels and historical sights, sporting activities and cable car.

Jurong Bird Park

More than 600 species of birds inhabit stunning landscaped settings. There is a waterfall and walking paths, as well as a panorail that leads to the aviaries.

Singapore Zoological Gardens

One of the world's finest zoos, it has open concept enclosures allowing animals to live in more natural settings. The Night Safari tour is a must.

Bukit Timah Nature Reserve

Home to exotic birds, monkeys and other wildlife, the reserve has various walking paths and superb views.

Singapore Botanic Gardens

Landscaped gardens are situated around lakes, wildlife, orchids, a Visitors Centre and various kiosks, cafes and some fine restaurants.

Fort Canning Park

Gothic gates, a Malay shrine, the island's first Christian cemetery, military ruins and the old British army barracks are some of the treasure in this park. Cultural performances, music and dance festivals are held here.

Raffles Hotel

Singapore's most famous colonial building serves the Singapore Sling that was created in the Long Bar in 1915. The Writer's Bar is located in the lobby.

Pulau Ubin

This offshore island can be reached by ferry from Changi Village. See how Malay and Chinese fishing communities lived in the 1960s, hire bicycles and enjoy wildlife and flora. There are seafood eating houses, overnight accommodation and campsites.

St John's Island

There are lagoons for swimming, walking paths and picnic areas. Arrive by ferry from the World Trade Centre. Some chalets are for rent here for those staying longer than a day.

OUTDOOR SPORTS

Singapore offers an array of water sporting activities, including scuba diving, water-skiing, wakeboarding, sailing, and windsurfing. For other challenging adventures such as abseiling, kayaking, BMX trail rides and trekking, the following clubs offer services for individuals and groups.

E-Factory

#02-5101, Block 10,
North Bridge Road, Singapore
ph: 6333 9950

Outward Bound Singapore

Pulau Ubin ph: 6545 9008

Singapore Adventure Club

74B Lorong 27, Geylang, Singapore
ph: 6749 0557

GOLF COURSES

Golf is becoming increasingly popular among visitors to Singapore and there are many world-class 18-hole courses on the island. Most are beautifully landscaped clubs with restaurants and pools that offer a day fee and clubs hire to non-members. Here are four– in the east, west,north and south.

Laguna National Golf & Country Club

11 Laguna Green, Singapore
ph: 6542 6888, 6541 0200

Raffles Country Club

450 Jalan Ahmad Ibrahim, Singapore
ph: 6861 7649, 6861 7655

The Seletar Base Golf Club

3 Park Lane, Seletar Air base, Singapore
ph: 6481 4745

Sentosa Golf club

27 Bukit Manis Road, Singapore
ph: 6275 0022

MUSEUMS

There are many excellent museums exhibiting Asian art collections, history and cultural traditions, and modern interactive technology. Home to the Performing Arts is the spectacular Esplanade, Theatres on the Bay, as well as Victoria Theatre, Kallang Theatre, Singapore Indoor Stadium, and Harbour Pavilion.

Asian Civilisations Museum

39 Armenian Street, Singapore
ph: 6332 3015

Singapore Art Museum

71 Bras Basah Road, Singapore
ph: 6332 3222

Singapore History Museum

93 Stamford Road, Singapore
ph: 6332 3659

Singapore Science Centre

15 Science Centre Road, Singapore
ph: 6425 2500

China Town